Key to the Symbols in This Book

 - avoid at all cost

 - just walk away

 - run away, screaming

 - exceedingly disgusting job

 - affords excellent opportunity
(for grave personal injury)

 - max out life insurance before accepting

 - don't just say no—say hell, no!

You Think Your Job
Stinks!

You Think Your Job Stinks!

Copyright © 2007 by Patrick Regan. All rights reserved. Printed in China. No part of
this book may be used or reproduced in any manner whatsoever without written
permission except in the case of reprints in the context of reviews. For information,
write Andrews McMeel Publishing, LLC, an Andrews McMeel Universal company,
4520 Main Street, Kansas City, Missouri 64111.

07 08 09 10 11 WKT 10 9 8 7 6 5 4 3 2 1

ISBN-13: 978-0-7407-5722-8
ISBN-10: 0-7407-5722-9

Library of Congress Control Number: 2005932780

www.andrewsmcmeel.com

Book design by Diane Marsh

ATTENTION: SCHOOLS AND BUSINESSES
Andrews McMeel books are available at quantity discounts with bulk purchase for
educational, business, or sales promotional use. For information, please write to:
Special Sales Department, Andrews McMeel Publishing, LLC, 4520 Main Street,
Kansas City, Missouri 64111.

You Think Your Job

Stinks!

Patrick Regan

**Andrews McMeel
Publishing, LLC**

Kansas City

Introduction

We all have rough days on the job. The work's piled high. The copier's jammed. The boss is on a tear. But before whining over your miserable lot in life, consider these questions: Did you wake up to the very real chance that you might be tattooing a pit bull today? Was "swallow a live rat" included on your to-do list? At any point in your day were you required to administer a (non-oral) laxative to a horse or wash a five-hundred-pound sumo wrestler's diaper?

Take heart, beleaguered worker. Things could be worse. This book, filled with real pictures of real people doing real jobs, is proof of that.

Deodorant Scent Tester

No way around it—this job is the pits.

Post Office
Mail Sorter

Fifty thousand letters a day . . .

and then you go home to a stack of bills.

Extreme Lawn Boy

One hell of a way to earn an allowance.

yuck!

Large Animal Vet

Yes, that's a horse's backside. Yes, he's wearing a shoulder-length vinyl glove, and yes, his entire arm is safe from the sun's harmful rays.

Human Cannonball

You soar 120 miles per hour, 100 feet through the air.

A member of a very small fraternity of courageous

acrobats, you are both daredevil and dedicated

entertainer. People lay down good money to see

if you'll miss the net and break your neck. With

alarming frequency, they are not disappointed.

Hazardous
Materials
Removal

Your job? To clean up toxins so lethal

that one whiff, one second of contact,

could rearrange your molecular structure.

Better wear the puffy coat.

Bike Messenger

STEP 1: Pick up unwieldy package from

rude receptionist.

STEP 2: Strap package to back.

STEP 3: Peddle furiously, sucking exhaust fumes,

dodging tourists, ignoring obscenities from

cab drivers.

STEP 4: Chain bike to pole. Drop off package to

rude receptionist.

STEP 5: Repeat until collapse.

Casket Maker

Forty years on the job, and not one lousy
time has a customer commented on the
craftsmanship and attention to detail.

yuck!

Sow
Inseminator

KNOW THIS: You will gain a nickname.

It will not be kind.

Concrete Finisher

The crippled knees aren't the worst part—or even
the grueling work in the blazing sun. The worst part
is that inevitable pack of stray dogs that runs
through every day just before quitting time.

Times Square Traffic Cop

Ah, Times Square—the crossroads of the world, the pulsing heart of the city that never sleeps. Your job? Stand in the middle of the street and resist the overwhelming urge to use deadly force.

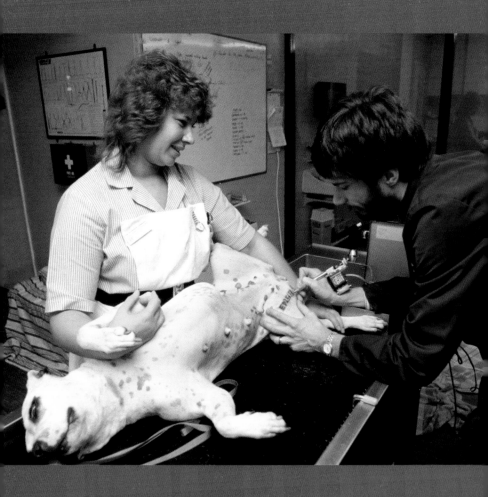

Pit Bull
Tattoo Artist

Better double-dose on the anesthesia, nurse.

Sideshow Freak

THE GOOD NEWS: You work in an underserved market with high job security.

THE BAD NEWS: You pretty much swallow rats all day.

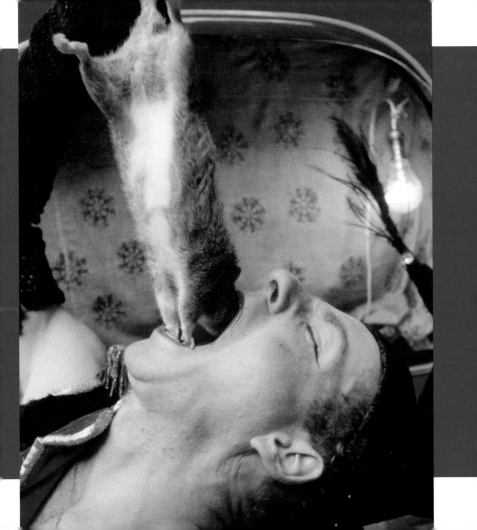

Bingo Caller

G-50 . . .

I-18 . . .

B-7 . . .

O . . . please someone shoot me now.

Vermin Control Agent

yuck!

A SUGGESTION: A job in which "rat tongs"

are standard issue is a job you might

consider passing on.

Alligator Wrestler

You'll know you've finally arrived in this sport

when you've earned a cool nickname like "Lefty"

or "Stubby" or "The Late, Great . . ."

Logging Truck Driver

According to the Bureau of Labor Statistics,

logging and trucking are two of the most

dangerous jobs in America. Congratulations!

You've hit the lethal job lotto!

yuck!

Mawashi Laundress

THE OBJECT OF SUMO: to move your opponent

to the ground or out of the ring.

THE CLASSIC METHOD: by grasping and pulling on

the opponent's mawashi (sumo diaper).

THE EFFECT: a wedgie of titanic proportions.

Now, who will washy mawashi?

Carnie

Step right up. Try your luck. See what I care.

help!

Bulletproof Vest Tester

Honestly, couldn't they just drape it over a

watermelon or something?

Struggling Stand-up Comic

There are no "sure things" in this wacky business,

but you can be nearly 100 percent certain that

executives from NBC are not going to be catching

your act at Leo's Laugh Hole in Akron, Ohio.

Iron Worker

ouch!

Hey, when the asbestos spoon melts down,

it's time for a smoke break!

help! Bull Rider

Let's see, 1,800-pound bull, 150-pound man. How can we make this a little more sporting? Oh, how about, he has to hold on with *one* hand.

Lost Baggage Handler

Congratulations. You will forever be remembered

as the lady who ruined Christmas.

Golden Gate Bridge Painter

How many times will this man hear,

"You missed a spot!" shouted at him from

a speeding car? Many, many times.

Wig Wrangler at Miss Fire Island Pageant

Do a good job with the wigs, and maybe, just maybe, you'll work your way up to handling the falsies.

Elephant Handler

Come on, what's the very worst thing that

could happen? Aside from being pooped on

and maybe kicked in the face?

Sidewalk
Performer

There is this thing called human dignity.

Never let it get in the way of a paying gig.

Photo Credits